CONTINENTS OF THE WORLD

Australia, Antarctica, and the Pacific

Kate Darian-Smith

WORLD ALMANAC® LIBRARY

Please visit our web site at: www.worldalmanaclibrary.com
For a free color catalog describing World Almanac® Library's list of high-quality books
and multimedia programs, call 1-800-848-2928 (USA) or 1-800-387-3178 (Canada).
World Almanac® Library's fax: (414) 332-3567.

Library of Congress Cataloging-in-Publication Data

Darian-Smith, Kate.
    Australia, Antarctica, and the Pacific / by Kate Darian-Smith.
        p. cm. — (Continents of the world)
    Includes bibliographical references and index.
    ISBN 0-8368-5912-X (lib. bdg.)
    ISBN 0-8368-5919-7 (softcover)
    1. Australia—Juvenile literature. 2. Antarctica—Juvenile literature.
    3. Oceania—Juvenile literature. I. Title. II. Series.
    DU96.D355 2005
    994—dc22   2005042110

This North American edition first published in 2006 by
World Almanac® Library
330 West Olive Street, Suite 100
Milwaukee, WI 53212 USA

This U.S. edition copyright © 2006 by World Almanac® Library. Original edition
copyright © 2005 by Hodder Wayland. First published in 2005 by Hodder Wayland,
an imprint of Hodder Children's Books, a division of Hodder Headline Limited,
338 Euston Road, London NW1 3BH, U.K.

Commissioning editor: Victoria Brooker
Editor: Katie Sergeant
Inside design: Jane Hawkins
Cover design: Hodder Wayland
Series concept and project management by
EASI-Educational Resourcing. (info@easi-er.co.uk)
Statistical research: Anna Bowden
World Almanac® Library editor: Barbara Kiely Miller
World Almanac® Library art direction: Tammy West
World Almanac® Library cover design: Dave Kowalski
World Almanac® Library production: Jessica Morris

Photo credits: Alamy 14; 17 (Irfan Parvez), 24 (Penny Tweedie), 31 (Sami Sarkis), 32 (Walter
Bibikow), 36 (Andy Christodolo), 38 (Doug Steley), 39 (Tim Graham); Ant Photo Library
15 (NHPA); Ardea 55 (Jean Paul Ferrero); The Art Archive 34 (Musée des Arts Africains et
Océaniens/A. Dagli Orti; Christine Osborne Pictures 33; Corbis cover, title page, 29, 49, 51,
58 (Reuters), 3, 6 (Owen Franken), 5 (Craig Tuttle), 7 (Mark A. Johnson) 10 (David Mercado/
Reuters), 12, 13 (Bettmann), 16 (Dennis Degnan), 18(b) (Jay Dickman), 21 (George D. Lepp),
23 (Paul A. Souders), 25 (Duomo), 27(t) (Bob Krist), 27(b) (Wolfgang Kaehler), 28 (Ted
Streshinsky), 30 (Nik Wheeler), 35 (Manuel Blondeau/Photo & Co.), 42 (Roger Garwood
and Trish Ainslie), 43 (Greg Smith), 44 (Catherine Karnow), 46 (Bob Krist), 47 (Staffan
Widstrand), 50 (Duomo), 53 (Kevin Fleming), 54 (Martin Harvey), 56 (Paul A. Souders),
57(t) (Tim Davis); Corbis Sygma 20 (Ed Chrisostomo), 45 (Durocher Christian); Ecoscene
37 (Wayne Lawler); Mary Evans Picture Library 9, 11; Eye Ubiquitous/Corbis 48 (Paul
Thompson), 52 (Matthew McKee); Getty Images 59 (The Image Bank); Nature Picture
Library 57(b) (Jurgen Freud); Science Photo Library 8; Still Pictures 18(t) (Doug Perrine),
40, 41 (Friedrich Stark). Maps and graphs: Martin Darlison, Encompass Graphics.
Population Density Map © 2003 UT-Battelle, LLC.

Printed in China

1 2 3 4 5 6 7 8 9 09 08 07 06 05

**The high volcanic peaks and coral-fringed
beaches of Bora Bora Island.**

CONTENTS

AUSTRALIA, ANTARCTICA, AND THE PACIFIC — REGION OF DIVERSITY

Australia is the world's smallest continent, with a landmass of 2,967,124 square miles (7,686,850 square kilometers). Australia's geographical remoteness means that it hosts many distinctive forms of animal and plant life. Much of the continent consists of low plateaus and arid deserts, but the majority of the population lives on the wetter, fertile plains in the south and east.

Antarctica is the world's fifth-largest continent and is located almost entirely within the Antarctic Circle, with the South Pole at its center. It covers approximately

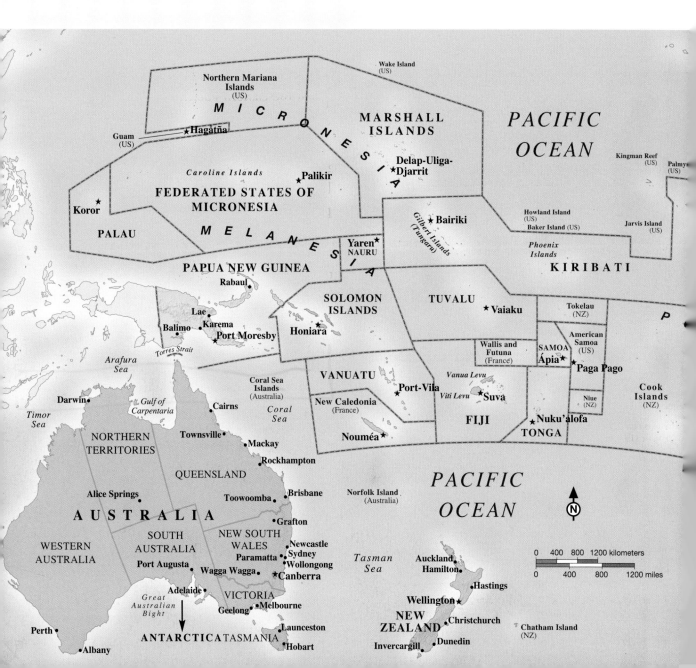

5,498,570 square miles (14,245,000 sq km) of which only 5 percent is ice-free. The remainder is covered by a continental ice sheet measuring approximately 7.2 million cubic miles (30 million cubic kilometers) and in some places is more than 1.25 miles (2 kilometers) thick. Antarctica does not contain any permanent human habitation, but it is important as a scientific station.

East of Australia is the Pacific Ocean, the massive body of water between the Southern Ocean, Asia, Australia, and the western hemisphere. The Pacific Ocean contains some 25,000 islands. Ten thousand of these islands in the tropical and subtropical areas of the central and South Pacific Ocean are known collectively as Oceania.

The Oceanic islands are divided into three groups on the basis of their similarities and differences in geography and the cultures of their peoples: Polynesia, Melanesia, and Micronesia. A population of 12.4 million people live on only 10 percent of these scattered islands. Melanesia is home to the majority (58.4 percent), with 5.5 million people located in Papua New Guinea alone.

Polynesia ("many islands") occupies a large part of the eastern Pacific Ocean between Hawaii, New Zealand, and Easter Island. Its many thousands of islands range from large volcanic formations to tiny coral atolls and are home to 4 million people or 38 percent of the population of Oceania.

Micronesia ("tiny islands") comprises more than 2,000 low-lying and coral islands. Only 3.1 percent of Oceania's population lives in Micronesia.

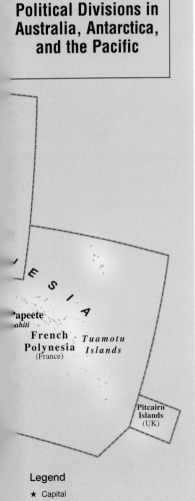

Political Divisions in Australia, Antarctica, and the Pacific

E S I A

apeete
ahiti
French Polynesia
(France)

Tuamotu Islands

Pitcairn
Islands
(UK)

Legend

★ Capital

• Major settlement

The coral-fringed beaches of Bora Bora Island are typical of many small islands in Polynesia.

5

1. THE HISTORIES OF AUSTRALIA, ANTARCTICA, AND THE PACIFIC

About 650–550 million years ago, the "supercontinent" Gondwanaland was made up of all the continents now located in the southern hemisphere: Australia, Antarctica, South America, and Africa, as well as the Indian Subcontinent. Gondwanaland gradually split up. A southern landmass with Australia at its core broke away some 45 million years ago and began to drift northward. As ocean levels rose at the end of the last ice age (about 12–8 million years ago), land bridges between Australia and what are now Papua New Guinea and New Zealand were flooded over.

Aitutaki Island of the Cook Islands was discovered by British Captain William Bligh of the ship HMS *Bounty* on April 11, 1789.

THE FIRST INHABITANTS

The human histories of the region are complex and dynamic. According to archaeologists, Australia's indigenous peoples, the Aborigines, have the longest continuous cultural history in the world. Australia has been inhabited for at least 50,000–60,000 years. Scientists think that the first settlers traveled by sea from Southeast Asia and over land bridges that connected Indonesia and New Guinea with Australia.

Parts of Melanesia were inhabited about 4,000 years ago by seafaring peoples from Southeast Asia and from the Fujian province of southern China. They gradually traveled from Melanesia into Polynesia and Micronesia, settling on the islands. By c. A.D. 800,

Polynesian seafarers, the ancestors of the Maori people, had reached New Zealand and established communities largely on its North Island.

EUROPEAN EXPLORATION

From ancient times, European cultures speculated that a "great southern continent" balanced the world. In A.D. 731, an English monk, the Venerable Bede, suggested that the poles were regions of eternal cold and that while the North Pole was ocean, the South Pole was a great land. In 1366, Sir John Mandeville, an English author of travel stories, was the first to use the word *Antarktyk* ("opposite the Arctic").

Between the fifteenth and seventeenth centuries, interest in the existence of a "great south land" was heightened by the

●●●●●●➤ IN FOCUS: Easter Island

On Easter Island, in the Pacific Ocean, about six hundred enormous stone statues and platforms, known as Moais, were carved from volcanic rock between A.D. 400 and 1600. Archaeologists are unsure what these monuments represented but believe they were erected by different tribes competing for land. The largest of the Moais is 39 feet (12 meters) tall. It would probably take about 100 people to move each Moais from the quarry where it was carved to its final resting place.

Some scholars think that the Easter Island statues represent the spirits of ancient chiefs and other important men.

competition between the seagoing European powers to "discover" new parts of the world. European explorers had already reached the Americas and Asia when sailors from Spain, Portugal, Britain, and France ventured farther into unchartered southern seas. In 1606, Dutch explorer Willem Jansz sighted northern Australia. In 1642, another Dutchman, Abel Tasman was the first to sight New Zealand, but hostility from the native people at Golden Bay, in the northeastern corner of New Zealand's South Island, prevented him from landing.

The most famous European explorer in the Pacific was an Englishman—Captain James Cook. His voyages mapped much of Melanesia and Polynesia, as well as the east coast of Australia. In 1768, Cook was sent by the British government to the island of Tahiti (now in French Polynesia) to view the transit of the planet Venus and then to explore the southern Pacific. In two further voyages, Cook made a circuit of the Pacific region south of the equator and established that New South Wales was, in fact, part of the continent of Australia.

EUROPEAN COLONIZATION IN AUSTRALIA AND OCEANIA

A British penal colony was established at Sydney Cove in New South Wales in 1788. The First Fleet (a group of eleven ships) sailed on an eight-month journey from England carrying convicts and government officers. In the first years at the settlement, the group endured hardship because of inadequate food supplies. The practice of transporting convicts to Australia continued until the 1840s in the eastern colonies and 1868 in Western Australia. It was not long, however, until "free immigrants" began to

Captain James Cook sailed on the *Endeavour* during his voyage of discovery in 1768–1771.

arrive. They were drawn by the promise of land and, by the 1850s, the discovery of gold.

As well as New South Wales, the separate British colonies of Tasmania, Victoria, South Australia, Western Australia, and Queensland were established on the Australian continent. The British claimed that they had a right to the land under the legal doctrine of *terra nullius* ("uninhabited land"), despite the presence of Aborigines. The indigenous peoples were driven from their traditional territories, with many violent clashes occurring between them and the settlers.

After 1790, European settlements were founded in New Zealand by whalers who first came from bases in Australia and later came directly from Britain, France, and the United States. The settlers were interested in products such as sealskin, timber, flax (a plant used to make linen), and whale oil. By 1840, the British government took possession of New Zealand to protect the interests of British whalers and sealers. British immigration to New Zealand grew, and towns sprang up. Tensions with the Maori, the indigenous landowners, quickly escalated into land wars in the 1850s and 1860s, resulting in the defeat of the indigenous peoples.

By the early nineteenth century, the European presence in Oceania was permanent. Political and territorial tensions in Europe contributed to the histories of the British, French, and German colonization. Traders and those who established plantations for tropical crops often preceded

FACT FILE

Many Aborigines died because they had no immunity to diseases introduced by European settlers, such as measles, smallpox, and even the common cold.

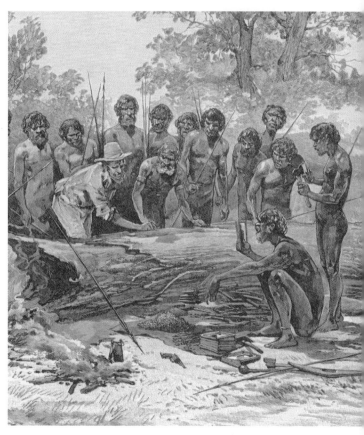

In 1835, settler John Batman offered a treaty to the Aboriginal owners of the site where the city of Melbourne was to be built. This treaty is not recognized as having any legal standing.

the formal territorial claims of European governments. There was a European scramble for the colonial possession of many of the Oceanic islands, and some islands have experienced successive waves of foreign colonization.

Britain took over many areas of interest in Oceania, including Fiji, the Solomon Islands, and a number of other smaller island groups. The French annexed various Polynesian island groups, including New Caledonia, Wallis and Futuna, and French Polynesia. In 1898, Germany purchased the islands of what is now the modern nation of the Federated States of Micronesia from Spain, their previous colonial power. These islands were to come under Japanese control in 1914.

Since 1828, the western half of New Guinea had been in the hands of the Dutch and remained so until 1963 when the United Nations sanctioned its transfer to Indonesia. In 1884, a German-owned trading company moved into the northeastern part of New Guinea. In reaction to this settlement, Britain and its Australian colonies seized Papua in the southeastern part of the island. In 1901, British New Guinea became an Australian territory, and beginning in 1920, German New Guinea was also under Australian rule. In fact, until its independence in 1975, an amalgamated Papua New Guinea was administered by Australia.

Sir Michael Somare was Papua New Guinea's first prime minister after it gained independence in 1975 and has served three terms as prime minister.

In 1820, American missionaries arrived in Hawaii and were soon followed by whalers and settlers. The Hawaiian monarchy was overturned in the early 1890s by American sugar planters. Hawaii was annexed by the United States in 1898, became a U.S. territory in 1900, and became a state in 1959. The U.S. naval base at Pearl Harbor on the island of Oahu, Hawaii, was established in 1908. By 1900, after a short war with Spain, the United States also had assumed control of Guam and other previous Spanish possessions in the islands of Micronesia.

INDEPENDENCE

In 1901, the separate British colonies in Australia federated to become one nation. The new Australia maintained the British monarch as its symbolic head of government and adopted the

IN FOCUS: Treaty of Waitangi

This treaty was regarded as the founding document of New Zealand and was signed in 1840 by five hundred Maori chiefs and a representative of the British government. The treaty was never officially approved by the British parliament, however, and had no legal validity. The British and Maori versions of the treaty were completely contradictory. The Waitangi Tribunal was established in 1976 to consider disputes relating to the treaty. By 2003, there had been eighteen settlements of historical treaty claims from Maori people, with a total value of almost US$430 million. Access to traditional food sources, including fishing rights, have now been returned to the Maori, and they have received property and cash in compensation for the loss of their land.

The Treaty of Waitangi was signed by five hundred Maori chiefs on May 21, 1840.

British system of parliament with an upper and lower house. New Zealand was declared an independent dominion of the British Empire in 1907.

Beginning in the 1960s, most of the island-nations of Oceania have gained some degree of political autonomy from the five foreign nations that administered them—the United Kingdom (U.K.), France, the United States, Australia, and New Zealand. Among this group, France and the United States have been the most resistant to support independence, largely due to their military interests in the Oceanic region.

WAR IN THE PACIFIC

The recent histories of some societies in Oceania have been affected by the fighting in the Pacific during World War II, because contact with American and Australian troops influenced local cultural and economic developments through exposure to Western attitudes and commodities. Japan's bombing of the United States' naval base at Pearl Harbor in Hawaii on December 7, 1941, brought the U.S. forces into World War II. Under the command of U.S. General Douglas MacArthur, U.S., Australian, and New Zealand troops fought

U.S. forces liberated the North Mariana island of Saipan from the Japanese on June 28, 1944.

against the Japanese on some Oceanic islands, including Papua New Guinea, the Mariana Islands, Guam, and Kiribati. The decisive Battle of the Coral Sea (May 4–8, 1942) and Battle of Midway (June 3–6, 1942), when U.S. forces repelled Japanese troops, took place in the Pacific.

ANTARCTIC EXPLORATION

Beginning in the early nineteenth century, various British, French, and American expeditions surveyed the frozen continent of Antarctica. The struggle inland to reach the geographic South Pole began with the 1901 expedition of Britain's Robert F. Scott. In January 1909, Australian Douglas Mawson reached the magnetic South Pole by sled, while a Norwegian expedition led by Roald Amundsen and Thorvald Nilsen was the first to reach the geographic South Pole on December 14, 1911. Scott and his companions arrived a month later but perished in a severe blizzard during the journey back to their base camp.

By the 1950s, expeditions to Antarctica were marked by international rivalry, resulting in the establishment of permanent scientific stations across Antarctica. In 1959, twelve nations with territorial interests in Antarctica, including Argentina, Australia, Chile, France, New Zealand, Norway, and the U.K., signed the Antarctica Treaty. This treaty set up a legal framework for the management of Antarctica. It permits scientific inquiry and forbids military operations or nuclear testing. Many other nations are now formally consulted about Antarctica's future.

FACT FILE

On February 7, 1821, American Captain John Davis became the first known person to land on Antarctica.

Norwegian explorers Roald Amundsen and Thorvald Nilsen check their bearings to confirm they have reached the South Pole.

2. AUSTRALIA, ANTARCTICA, AND THE PACIFIC ENVIRONMENTS

*T*OGETHER AUSTRALIA, ANTARCTICA, AND OCEANIA COVER massive land and sea areas and encompass extraordinarily diverse and extreme environmental conditions. Antarctica's frozen plateaus contrast with the balmy tropics of the Pacific. Australia's water-starved and barren deserts stand out against its lush tropical rain forests. The coral atolls of the Pacific islands belie the region's volcanic mountains, which are often hidden by low-lying clouds.

AUSTRALIA: "THE DRY CONTINENT"

The landmass of Australia extends over 33° of latitude, one-third of which lies between the equator and the Tropic of Capricorn. It is an ancient land, with some rock formations dating back at least 3 billion years.

More than 60 percent of Australia's terrain is dominated by arid to semiarid low plateaus and great deserts where the average annual rainfall is less than 12 inches (300 millimeters). The lowest rainfall recorded is at Lake Eyre with less than 6 inches (150 mm) per annum. This lake is generally a dry saltpan and is only filled with water every few years.

The highest temperature ever recorded in Australia of 127° Fahrenheit (52.7° Celsius) was in 1889 at Cloncurry, in inland Queensland. The lowest temperature of –3° F (–19° C) was recorded at Charlotte Pass in the Snowy

Dead fish at Australia's Lake Eyre after its waters have dried up.

FACT FILE

Although Antarctica is the driest continent, Australia is the driest inhabited continent in the world.

The Murray-Darling river system is a major waterway that stretches over 2,300 miles (3,700 km) from Queensland to South Australia. The Murray River flows from the Snowy Mountains to the Great Australian Bight, on South Australia's coast. Its main tributaries are the Darling, Murrumbidgee, and Goulburn Rivers. The "mighty" Murray passes through Australia's main wheat and sheep producing regions, as well as irrigated areas where cotton, rice, citrus fruits, and grapes are grown. The Murray River also provides the water needs of many towns as well as the city of Adelaide. The overuse of water in the Murray-Darling river system has damaged the habitation of waterbirds, wetlands, and flood plains. It has also

resulted in increasing salinity within the soil. But farming along the Murray supports dozens of small towns, thousands of jobs, and hundreds of millions of dollars in economic growth. The Murray-Darling Basin Commission has been established by the government to manage the use of Australia's major river system and to examine how environmental sustainability can be achieved.

The Murray River originates in Australia's spectacular Snowy Mountains.

Mountains. Droughts occur regularly in Australia, as do flash floods that follow periods of sudden and heavy rain.

Australia's red and yellow-brown, sandy-soiled deserts host a vegetation of spinifex, cane grass, and saltbushes and are home to animals and insect life acclimatized to the extreme temperatures and arid conditions, such as snakes, termites, and lizards, including large goannas. At the edges of the desert are semiarid areas of mallee (dwarf eucalyptus) and mulga (acacia) scrub. Here the tree forms are bushy with

FACT FILE

The Gibson Desert, Great Victorian Desert, Great Sandy Desert, and Nullarbor Plain are Australia's largest deserts and together spread across large parts of Western Australia, South Australia, and the Northern Territory.

FACT FILE

The highest point in Australia is Mount Kosciusko in the Snowy Mountains, at 7,310 feet (2,228 m).

many branching trunks that may form a dense canopy that protects rodents, such as jerba-rats, small hare-wallabies, rat-kangaroos, and reptiles from large predators.

The central highlands regions in the eastern and northern parts of Australia make up more than one-quarter of the continent. Here the flat, semiarid scrub gives way to mountain ranges and savanna grasslands. Annual seasonal rains produce carpets of multicolored annual flowers and herbs.

The highland region of the eastern coastline makes up 15 percent of Australia and is dominated by the Great Dividing Range of mountains. The climate ranges from temperate in the southern half of the highland region to tropical in the northern half. The tropical north also receives the highest rainfalls. The wettest recorded location in Australia is Tully in Northern Queensland with an average rainfall of 170 inches (4,300 mm).

Sixty percent of Australia relies on ground water (such as lakes, pools, and runoff) and underground water, particularly the Great Artesian Basin. The basin stretches through Queensland to South Australia and is the largest body of underground water in the world. But overuse, particularly for livestock watering, has greatly exceeded the natural replenishment through its internal drainage system, causing the level of the basin to drop. As a consequence, many bores, or wells, have run dry or require pumping. These issues are being addressed through conservation efforts.

Millaa Millaa Falls is located in northern Queensland and is a popular site for swimming.

FACT FILE

The Great Artesian Basin was discovered in the 1880s and made settlement in inland Australia possible.

THE ISLANDS OF OCEANIA

Oceania's islands have a variety of landforms, soils, and plant and animal life. They are divided into continental and oceanic islands.

Continental islands are largely high mountainous islands with rich soils, located on the now partly submerged continental shelf that stretches along the western Pacific Ocean and that links Asia and Australia. This shelf covers 342,000 square miles (885,780 sq km) and measures 1,500 miles (2,415 km) long and 400 miles (645 km) at its widest. New Guinea's vast mountain ranges, such as the snowcapped Owen Stanley and Bismarck Mountains, are about 16,400-feet (5,000-m) high, while the low coastal plains are either swampy or densely forested. New Zealand is also predominantly mountainous with some coastal plains. Aoraki-Mount Cook is its highest mountain at 12,316 feet (3,754 m).

Mount Cook National Park on New Zealand's South Island was declared a national park in 1953.

Oceanic islands are split between the high, volcanic islands of Polynesia and Micronesia and low coral atolls with reefs that make up the majority of Pacific islands. On these coral islands, which have been built up by coral reef deposits over millions of years, the lowest point is often at sea level. These islands contrast strongly with the dense, basalt volcanic outcroppings that rise thousands of feet

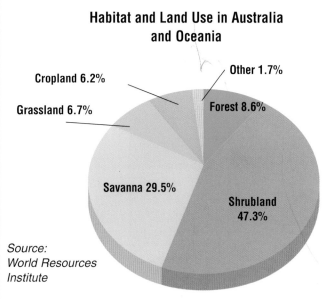

Habitat and Land Use in Australia and Oceania

Cropland 6.2%
Grassland 6.7%
Other 1.7%
Forest 8.6%
Savanna 29.5%
Shrubland 47.3%

Source:
World Resources
Institute

17

Mauna Kea, on the Big island of Hawaii, is the highest island mountain in the world, rising about 32,000 feet (9,750 m) from the Pacific Ocean floor and 13,796 feet (4,205 m) above sea level.

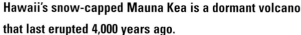

Hawaii's snow-capped Mauna Kea is a dormant volcano that last erupted 4,000 years ago.

out of the sea, such as French Polynesia's Mont Orohena, at 7,352 feet (2,241 m), or Hawaii's now dormant, snow-capped Mauna Kea.

The islands on the continental plateau generally are more fertile than volcanic or coral ocean islands. Over time, their size, geological age, and climate have combined to enrich the soils with nutrients and minerals. The amount of productive land is limited, however, due to their mountain ranges and is usually found on the lower mountain slopes or alluvial plains. Fiji, for example, is 7,052 square miles (18,270 sq km) in size, but only 12 percent is arable land.

Coral islands suffer other limitations, too. One is their small size. Another is the leaching of nutrients by heavy rainfall, reducing the fertility of the soil. Farmers are forced to use fertilizers or leave the land unused for a long period of time to allow the soil to regenerate. Associated environmental problems include soil erosion, which has been hastened by rapid deforestation, as is occurring in the Solomon Islands.

Many economies in Oceania have been forced to seek revenue through the introduction of industries that damage the environment, such as the cutting down of forests.

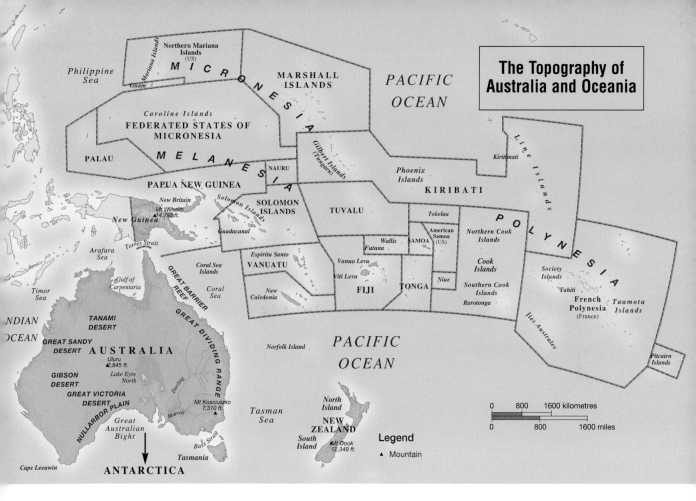

Another problem facing most islands is the lack of fresh
water. Despite high rainfalls, most of them do not have
large catchment areas to retain freshwater. Consequently,
governments, such as American Samoa's, have to invest
a lot of money improving water catchment and pipelines.

CLIMATE IN OCEANIA

The climate of Oceania is uniformly tropical with high
humidity and heavy rainfall all year round. The regional
differences that occur are the result of altitude, air circu-
lation patterns, and the time of the year. From November
to March, the western slopes of islands, such as the Solomon Islands and New Guinea, receive monsoonal rains
that are carried by the northwest monsoon from Asia.
During summer months, the southeast monsoon brings
rain to the islands' eastern slopes.

FACT FILE

The mountainous island
of New Guinea is the
world's second-largest
island after Greenland.

Seasonal weather is also responsible for the typhoons, or hurricanes, that often occur in western Micronesia from July to November. These storms bring severe winds, torrential rain, and high waves. They cause extensive damage to crops and buildings, especially on low-lying coral islands.

Typhoons, such as the one that struck Guam in 1997, regularly leave devastation in their wake.

EL NIÑO
The most destructive climatic phenomenon in the region is El Niño. It is a disruption of the ocean-atmosphere system that occurs in the tropical Pacific Ocean but which has consequences on global climatic conditions. During El Niño, the trade winds in the central and western Pacific lose their strength, resulting in an unusual rise in the temperature of the ocean and irregular patterns of rainfall and atmospheric currents. As a consequence, marine life is affected, and the atmospheric changes can cause destructive storms and hurricanes in the Pacific and severe drought in parts of Australia, too.

FACT FILE

Antarctica's mountain ranges have altitudes of up to 16,410 feet (5,000 m).

ANTARCTICA
Antarctica is the highest continent on Earth, with an average land height of 6,560 feet (2,000 m). The highest mountain is Vinson Massif at 16,067 feet (4,897 m). In contrast, the lowest known land point is hidden in the Bentley Subglacial Trench, at 8,382 feet (2,555 m) below sea level. This point is the deepest ice yet discovered and the world's lowest elevation not under seawater.

The Circum-Antarctic Current is the world's largest ocean current. It circulates clockwise around the entire Antarctic continent and is associated with a system of prevailing westerly winds that encircle the globe at latitudes between 40 and 60 degrees, known as the Roaring Forties, Furious Fifties, and Screaming Sixties.

Antarctica is the coldest, windiest, highest, and driest continent on Earth. The lowest temperature ever recorded on Earth is $-129°$ F ($-89.4°$ C) in 1983 at Vostok. The strongest winds were recorded at D'Urville and measured 233 miles per hour (375 kilometers per hour). The average rainfall that falls on the polar plateau is less than 2 inches (50 mm) per year.

During summer in the southern hemisphere, the South Pole receives more direct solar radiation from the Sun than anywhere else on the planet. Consequently, the greatest environmental threat to Antarctica is the ozone hole covering the region, which in 1998 was identified by NASA as the largest on record, covering 10 million sq miles (27 million sq km). The ultraviolet light coming through the hole is damaging ice, fish and marine plants and is causing the disintegration of significant areas of ice shelves.

The Alimirante Brown research station at Pacific Bay in Antarctica is maintained by Argentina.

3. THE PEOPLES OF AUSTRALIA, ANTARCTICA, AND THE PACIFIC

*A*N ESTIMATED 32.4 MILLION PEOPLE LIVE AND WORK IN AUSTRALIA, OCEANIA, and Antarctica. The majority are of European descent, and their migration to the region over the past two centuries has dramatically altered its ethnic and cultural profile. Australia and New Zealand, as former settler colonies of Britain, have been the leading destinations for millions of immigrants from Britain and increasingly from other parts of Europe, Asia, and the United States. Recent decades, however, have also seen an increased pattern of internal migration within the region itself.

AUSTRALIA'S PEOPLE

Australia's population is about 20 million. During the first 150 years of colonial settlement, about 98 percent of immigrants came from the British Isles, with a large proportion from Ireland. The gold rush of the

FACT FILE

Antarctica has no permanent inhabitants, but approximately 4,000 scientists, support staff, and naval crews stay there for limited periods of time throughout the year.

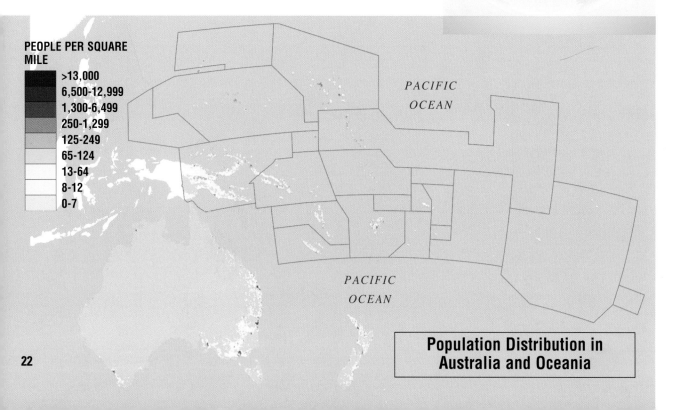

PEOPLE PER SQUARE MILE
- >13,000
- 6,500-12,999
- 1,300-6,499
- 250-1,299
- 125-249
- 65-124
- 13-64
- 8-12
- 0-7

PACIFIC OCEAN

PACIFIC OCEAN

Population Distribution in Australia and Oceania

1850s, however, attracted thousands of miners from China as well as from many parts of Europe and the United States. In 1947, with a population of just 7 million, Australia launched a massive immigration program to boost its population numbers and, thereby, aid economic development. In succeeding decades, waves of immigrants have arrived from northern, central, and southern Europe, the Middle East, and, more recently, from Asia, particularly Vietnam and China. Australia's discriminatory "White Australia" immigration policy, passed by federal legislation in 1901, was formally abandoned in 1973. The policy aimed to stop the immigration of non-Europeans to Australia through bureaucratic means. An official policy of multiculturalism has now been adopted, which recognizes the value of cultural diversity.

Almost 25 percent of the people living in Australia in 2004 were born overseas. Australia is, proportionally, second only to Israel in terms of being an "immigrant nation." While English remains the official language, more than one hundred other languages are spoken in Australian homes. The city of Melbourne has the third-largest Greek-speaking population in the world, outside Athens and Thessaloniki. Ethnic social clubs, places of worship, and shops are found in all Australian cities. About 7 percent of the population is of Asian origin, and this proportion is rising.

The largest group of immigrants to Australia in recent years, however—almost 20 percent annually—have come from Oceania, primarily from New Zealand. Australia remains committed to admitting immigrants under particular programs, such as family reunion, and prefers immigrants with occupation or business skills that are seen to meet national

Children from Melbourne's large Greek community are dressed in traditional national costumes to celebrate Greek Independence Day on March 25.

interests. While Australia also supports the immigration of refugees on humanitarian grounds, there have been recent measures to deter those entering the country illegally, including holding illegal immigrants or refugees in detention centers until their applications for immigration can be officially processed. The Australian government has also not recognized many recent claims for refugee status made by potential immigrants.

INDIGENOUS PEOPLES IN AUSTRALIA

Australia has two groups of indigenous peoples: Aborigines who live on the Australian mainland and in Tasmania and Torres Strait Islanders whose traditional lands are in the islands of Torres Strait off the Cape York Peninsula in northern Australia. It is estimated that before European colonization, the indigenous populations numbered between 750,000 and 3 million. They occupied about five hundred different territories and spoke hundreds of distinct languages, although the majority of these have now disappeared.

Todd Conde, pictured here with his mother Lismore, is editor of the *Koori Mail*, the national newspaper for Aborigine and Torres Strait Islander people.

In 1967, Aborigine and Torres Strait Islander peoples were granted the same citizenship rights as other Australians. Land rights has become a major political issue, and some lands have been "returned" to the Aborigines. In 1992, a High Court decision overturned the concept of *terra nullius*, under which the British had settled in Australia. Aboriginal communities must now provide evidence of their prior occupation of the land, and the legal processes are complex. Many Aboriginal communities in remote areas, however, now enjoy some degree of economic independence. Many other Aborigines live in Australia's cities and towns.

The 2001 national census figures show that the indigenous population in Australia numbers about 2.5 percent (approximately 458,500), but the numbers are rising. The birth rate of Native people is higher than that of other Australians, but the average age of mortality is noticeably lower, with health among the Aborigine population being a major social issue. Sadly, the death rate of Australia's indigenous people is double that of nonindigenous people, and their average life expectancy is approximately 20 years lower than that for the nonindigenous population. The main health concerns of indigenous people are related to issues of poverty and inadequate healthcare services, particularly in rural areas.

Cathy Freeman, an indigenous Australian athlete, won international acclaim after winning a gold medal at the 2000 Olympics in Sydney .

NEW ZEALAND'S PEOPLES

In 2004, approximately 79.1 percent of New Zealand's 4 million people were of European, predominantly British, descent (referred to by the Maori as "Pakeha") and the largest European settlement in Oceania. The Maori make up 9.7 percent of the population, 3.8 percent are Pacific Islanders, and 7.4 percent are Asian.

FACT FILE

The official bilingual name of New Zealand is "New Zealand/Aotearoa." Aotearoa is the Maori name for the nation and means "land of the long white cloud." The country's official emblem is the kiwi bird.

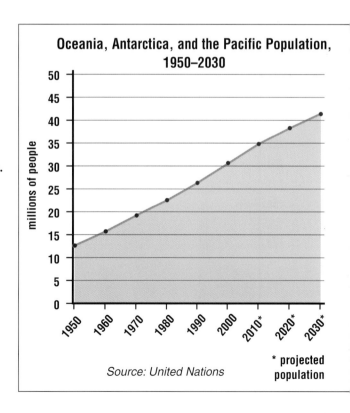

Oceania, Antarctica, and the Pacific Population, 1950–2030

Source: United Nations

* projected population

New Zealand has adopted a policy of biculturalism, with both English and Maori as the official languages and Maori now being taught in schools. About 200,000 Maori lived in New Zealand in 1769, the year they first had contact with Europeans. By 1896, European colonization had reduced their numbers to 42,000, but since the middle of the twentieth century, the Maori population has increased considerably to about 390,000 people in 2004.

URBAN NATIONS

Both Australia and New Zealand are highly urbanized nations. For more than a century, people have drifted from rural areas to cities for employment, education, and economic reasons and opportunities. Approximately 88 percent of Australia's population now lives in cities and large towns. The cities on the country's eastern seaboard—Brisbane, Sydney, and Melbourne—account for almost half of the national population. Eighty percent of the people in New Zealand also live in cities and towns. Both Australian and New Zealand cities are distinguished by the continuing spread of their suburbs.

The depopulation of rural areas in Australia has resulted in the loss of services, such as banks and medical clinics, in some towns. But this trend may be reversing. The fastest growing regions in Australia are smaller, commuter, and "lifestyle" towns along the coast and inland from the major cities. Foreign ownership of land in Australia and New Zealand, especially along the coastline, has become a concern for local populations. Maori communities, for example, fear that this shift in ownership will lead to the loss of their access to traditional lands.

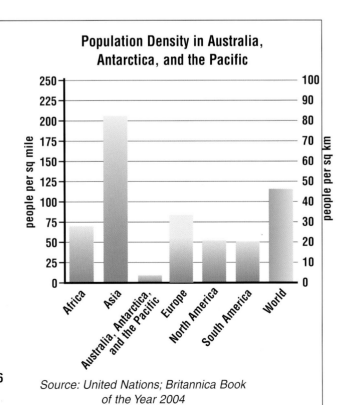

Population Density in Australia, Antarctica, and the Pacific

Source: United Nations; Britannica Book of the Year 2004

OCEANIA'S PEOPLES

The peoples who live in the Oceanic groups of Micronesia, Melanesia, and Polynesia are enormously diverse in their cultures. Indeed, 1,200 of the world's 6,800 languages are spoken by the 7 million people who live in Oceania. New Guinea alone has 715 indigenous languages, while Polynesia has 20 and Micronesia another 13.

The marrow of the sago palm tree is a staple in the diet of villagers in Papua New Guinea.

The largest number of indigenous peoples live in Melanesia, particularly on Papua New Guinea (with a population of approximately 5.4 million), Fiji (approximately 900,000), and Solomon Islands (approximately 523,000). Polynesia has the second largest population (approximately 684,000, excluding Hawaii). Polynesians, as well as the people living in Micronesia, are dispersed over many islands, with the number of people on each island varying from a few hundred to tens of thousands. The 21,000 inhabitants of the Cook Islands, for example, are dispersed over seven low-lying, infertile, and sparsely populated coral atolls and eight volcanic islands that support the majority of people.

FACT FILE

Pitcairn Island has the smallest population in Oceania, with only about fifty people. The population has declined due to the lack of freshwater and the need for people to leave the island for work or study.

Most people living on Oceanic islands continue to live in rural and fishing communities, often in small villages with limited opportunities for employment.

Net fishing in shallow waters is a primary source of food for many Micronesian villagers.

FACT FILE

More people from the Cook Islands and Niue actually live in New Zealand than in their own countries.

The rising population growth rate in many Oceanic nations (between 1 and 2 percent each year) has caused serious issues of overpopulation. Kiribati's 100,800 people, for example, are spread over 21 of the 33 small coral atolls and place a strain on the few available resources.

The limitations of space, resources, and employment have meant that increasing numbers of people within Oceania are moving to urban centers or migrating to New Zealand and the French- and United States-controlled nations.

Immigration and settlement from Europe, Asia, and the United States have changed the demographic profile of many Oceanic island-nations. In addition to residents with European ancestry, Hawaii has a large number of immigrants from the U.S. mainland, China, Japan, Korea, and the Philippines. New Caledonia has had an influx of French as well Chinese, Vietnamese, and Indonesian immigrants. Forty-four percent of Fiji's population of 900,000 are Indo-Fijian. These people are the descendants of indentured laborers from the Indian Subcontinent who were brought to Fiji during the colonial period to work on the sugar plantations.

Hawaii's cultural diversity is seen in this Buddhist temple that was converted into a museum in 1985.

EDUCATION IN THE REGION

Australia and New Zealand have education systems equal in standard to those in other Western, developed nations. Their university systems are internationally acclaimed and attract many students from Asia, the United States, and the Oceanic region.

Educational opportunities in some Oceanic nations are limited. Overall, however, literacy levels are improving, and regional higher education institutions, such as the multicampus University of the South Pacific, have played an important role in providing professional training.

FACT FILE

Eighty percent of Australian high school students enroll in higher education at universities or colleges. This level of higher education is only surpassed in the United States and Canada.

• • • • • • ▶ IN FOCUS: Fiji

Conflict between different ethnic groups has led to political and economic instability in Fiji. In 1970, Fiji gained independence from Britain but remained a member of the British Commonwealth. In 1987, Sitiveni Rabuka, a colonel in the Fijian army, led two military coups against the government, which was dominated by Fijians of Indian descent (Indo-Fijians). He proclaimed Fiji a republic, severing ties to the Commonwealth. By early 1988, the country returned to civilian rule, but violence and tension between Fijians and Indo-Fijians continued. On May 19, 2000, a civilian coup was executed by radical indigenous Fijians who ousted Fiji's first ethnic Indian government led by Prime Minister Chaudry.

Indigenous Fijians were concerned about proposed land reforms and possible social justice laws. In 2004, Indo-Fijians continued to be denied a share of the political power and suffered social, economic, and educational discrimination. The government has attempted to heal the political and racial instability by calling for national prayer meetings involving the Christian, Hindu, and Muslim populations and for public demonstrations of patriotism, such as flying the national flag.

Fijian nationalists march on Parliament House in May 2000 to show support for the military coup.

4. CULTURE AND RELIGION IN AUSTRALIA AND THE PACIFIC

MIGRATION AND SETTLEMENT FROM EUROPE AND THE UNITED States into Australia and Oceania have deeply influenced the cultural, religious, and social facets of traditional life in the region.

THE MISSIONARIES AND CHRISTIANITY

The preaching of evangelical Protestant and Roman Catholic missionaries among Oceanic peoples began in 1798, when the London Missionary Society first arrived on Tahiti. As a result of continued evangelical efforts, Christianity has become the dominant religion in Oceania. Almost the entire population of Western Samoa, for example, is officially Christian. In some cases, localized Christian denominations have developed, as with the Cook Islands Christian Church.

Christianity is widely practiced in Oceania, and churches like this one on the Cook Islands are numerous.

The influence of missionaries and European settlers brought about changes in the traditional lifestyles of people in Oceania, such as alternative agricultural methods and the introduction of Western clothing. In many cases, however, traditional beliefs and kinship systems have been integrated into Westernized forms of social, political, and economic life.

TRADITIONAL BELIEFS IN OCEANIA

Traditional lifestyles, religions, and societies in the island-nations of Oceania are very diverse. In general terms, Oceanic religions worshiped many gods, and these beliefs are present in everyday activities and artistic practices. A close relationship existed between the living and the spirits of ancestors.

Oceanic mythology was passed down by oral tradition through many generations. Their complex stories tell of gods and spirits who are linked to places of symbolic significance. Adaro, the sea spirit, appears in many Polynesian and Melanesian myths. Some myths explain the existence of the sea as the sweat of the spiritual parent and god of the oceans, Tangaroa, as he created the world.

In some places in Melanesia, traditional religious beliefs are still practiced.

KINSHIP IN OCEANIA

The ties that link the individual, the family, and the community are known as kinship relationships. These are extremely important in traditional Oceanic cultures and determine all political and social structures. Kinship relationships are often maintained through the exchange of foodstuffs and tokens, such as shells, beads, and feathers, and are marked by ritual ceremonies.

In many societies, there is a strict hierarchy based on birthright and political importance. In Polynesian and Micronesian societies, the position of chief is inherited and is supported through *mana,* or personal power. A number of modern independent Polynesian states only permit those who are chiefs to hold positions in parliament. In Tonga, civil war broke out following the arrival of British missionaries. In 1845, a strong chief united the people and was crowned king, establishing a hereditary monarchy.

FACT FILE

Despite being firmly tied to the United States, in the Federated States of Micronesia, men wear loincloths and still use stone coins as currency, while ties and baseball caps have been banned.

FACT FILE

Tonga has the only constitutional monarchy in Oceania.

Ritual body tattooing is done in elaborate and complex designs.

ARTISTIC LIFE IN OCEANIA

In some traditions, it is believed that sea god Tangaroa had human children, one of whom, Rua-te-pupuke, is said to have discovered the art of carving, a skill that became central to Oceanic culture. Art in Oceania is not produced for the sake of art itself but for a particular political, social, or religious function, such as the appeasement of gods or spirits. Oceanic visual art makes use of a great range of commonplace materials found in the natural environment. The materials, the final product, and the symbolic decorations vary enormously from community to community. Thus, masks are worn in Melanesia but not Micronesia. Another medium for Oceanic art is the human body. The bluish-black tattoos worn by men and women in Polynesia, and to a lesser degree in Micronesia and Melanesia, announce physical maturity or prowess in battle.

Ornaments further serve as a mark of an individual's rank and wealth and include necklaces, ear and nose rings, and leg and arm bands made from shells, bones, and whale and other fish teeth. Among Melanesian and Polynesian men, clamshell and turtle-shell disks are worn as a necklace pendant or on a band around the forehead. In New Zealand, colored feathers are woven into cloaks worn by men and women of high tribal rank.

STORYTELLING AND LITERATURE IN OCEANIA

Throughout Oceania, storytelling is very important, and histories and other stories are told through oral traditions. The focus is on song and dance, which are performed as a means of telling stories. In Melanesia, for example, dancers wearing elaborate costumes and masks describe the activities of gods and ancestors.

Traditional Oceanic societies had no written language. Today, there are written versions of the major languages, and English is widely taught in the school system. In the 1970s and 1980s, a "Pacific" literature, written in English, began to be published. Writers such as Samoa's Albert Wendt have achieved recognition for fictional works that blend traditional forms of storytelling with an exploration of contemporary society.

RELIGION IN AUSTRALIA AND NEW ZEALAND

In Australia, Christianity remains the predominant religious group and represents approximately 76 percent of the population. Islam is the fastest growing religion, reflecting the recent trend of immigration from the Middle East and parts of Asia. In New Zealand, the various Christian denominations (especially Anglicanism and Presbyterianism) account for 64 percent of religious belief.

THE ABORIGINAL DREAMTIME

Traditional Aborigine society has a complex system of social, spiritual, and cultural laws that are connected to the land. Aborigines believe that the creation of the world occurred during the Dreamtime, when ancestral spirits brought all plants, animals, rivers, and mountains into existence. Dreamtime creation stories

Islam is the fastest growing religion in Australia. Gallipoli Mosque, *below*, is one of several mosques in Sydney.

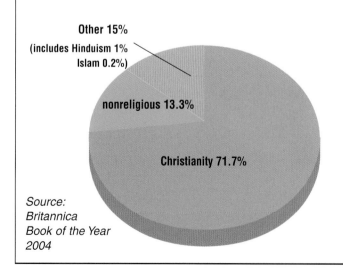

Religions in Australia and Oceania

Other 15%
(includes Hinduism 1%
Islam 0.2%)

nonreligious 13.3%

Christianity 71.7%

Source:
Britannica
Book of the Year
2004

This Aboriginal bark painting depicts the body. It was painted by artist Lipundja of Milingimbi, Australia.

are passed on orally, through dancing, singing, in ceremonies, and in forms of visual art. Within Aboriginal spiritual beliefs, every meaningful activity, event, or life process that occurs at a particular place leaves behind something of itself, which then shapes some part of the land—rocks, riverbeds, water holes. These places then assume significance as "sacred sites." Aboriginal culture maintains and adapts the laws that were laid down in the Dreamtime.

ABORIGINAL ART

Traditional Aboriginal art varied enormously throughout Australia, depending on the availability of materials and the practices of each group. Visual representation of Dreamtime stories was made on rocks, on large sheets of bark, and on bodies for ceremonies. Since the 1970s, there has been increasing national and international recognition of the work of contemporary Aboriginal artists. Dreamtime stories are visually told using modern materials, such as canvas and acrylic paint. Aboriginal art and performance has added considerably to Australia's cultural and tourist industries. In addition, sales of artworks have provided Aboriginal communities with a source of income.

CLEVER NATIONS

Australia and New Zealand are often referred to as "clever nations" because of the literary, artistic, and scientific achievements of their small populations. Both nations have vigorous national literature canons, with many authors, such as Nobel prize winner Patrick White of Australia and Janet Frame of New Zealand, receiving international acclaim and prizes. Australia is recognized around the world for its innovation in the fields of agricultural research and biotechnology. Several Australians have won Nobel prizes for scientific advances in medicine, chemistry, and physics, and Australian technology is highly competitive internationally.

●●●●●●➤ IN FOCUS: Sports in Australia and New Zealand

Sports are important social and cultural activities throughout Oceania. Many of the games played were introduced to the region by the British in the nineteenth century. Australia and New Zealand have long enjoyed international recognition for their sporting prowess in a range of sports, including cricket, rugby, swimming, surfing, and tennis. Australia is also the home of its own football code, Australian Rules Football, a game that is based on both Irish and Aboriginal sports traditions. "Aussie Rules" is a game that relies on excellent ball handling and kicking skills and great endurance, with players running as many as 12–19 miles (20–30 km) during a game.

Australia and New Zealand compete in the 2003 Rugby World Cup series.

5. NATURAL RESOURCES IN AUSTRALIA, ANTARCTICA, AND THE PACIFIC

OCEANIA AND ANTARCTICA ARE RICH IN NATURAL RESOURCES that have been vigorously sought by individuals, companies, and multinational organizations. This aggressive and, sometimes, greedy exploitation, however, has often severely damaged the landscapes and natural life of the region.

Wind-driven pumps are used to access underground sources of water.

FACT FILE

Ninety percent of irrigation projects in Australia have been built by and are controlled by the government.

WATER: THE MOST PRECIOUS RESOURCE

By the end of the nineteenth century, most of the land in Australia had been taken by white settlers for grazing, agriculture, and mining. Approximately 60 percent of the Australian continent is used for farming, and most of this is for grazing. In the drier regions, vast grazing properties often stretched over thousands of square miles (kilometers). European farming methods were often unsuitable for the Australian environment, and specialized farming equipment was invented, such as the stump-jump plow, which was used to jump over obstacles like old tree stumps and rocks. The development of Australia's agricultural and grazing industries, however, was dependent on the availability of the continent's most precious resource—water.

Less than 10 percent of the continent is naturally suited for growing crops. As a result, about 3 million acres (1.2 million hectares) of cultivated land is under irrigation

36

in Australia, enabling the growth of vegetables, fruit, cotton, and rice. Irrigation is often costly, however, and drains large amounts of water away from river systems. Cubbie Station in Queensland, for example, relies on the damming of the Condamine-Balonne river system. A giant storage dam is used to irrigate just 34,600 acres (14,000 ha) of cotton production.

Through intensive grazing and agriculture, settlers have dramatically reshaped and in some cases mismanaged Australia's physical environment. One major problem is soil erosion. It is caused by the removal of vegetation through overgrazing and damage to the soil from the hooves of cattle and sheep.

In recent decades, a growing awareness of the need for water and soil conservation has occurred in Australia. Government-sponsored programs have encouraged farmers to plant more trees and care for their land, but the problem of water management remains pressing.

FACT FILE

Sixty percent of all Australian soils now require treatment for erosion or salinity, the latter of which has been caused by rising salt levels in artesian water that drains into soils.

MINERAL AND ENERGY RESOURCES IN AUSTRALIA

Australia is rich in a broad range of natural resources, including bauxite, coal, iron ore, tin, gold, silver, uranium, nickel, tungsten, diamonds, natural gas, and petroleum. In 2003–2004, the value of Australia's minerals and energy exports were valued at US$33 billion (or 31 percent of export earnings).

Erosion caused by winds and water run-off is a major environmental problem.

The discovery of gold in the 1850s led to the birth of Australia's mining industry. Australia continues to mine about 10 percent of the world's supply of gold. Heavy machinery and deep tunnels in places such as Kalgoorlie have now replaced the difficult and dangerous work of those early miners. In 2003, gold was worth US$4.5 billion as an export commodity, second only to coal (US$8.4 billion).

Australia has become the world's largest producer of bauxite, which is used to make aluminum, as well as contributing heavily to the world's supply of iron ore and uranium, a raw material used for generating nuclear power. This extensive mining contributes heavily to Australia's GDP and employment.

Aluminum ore, called bauxite, is most commonly formed in deeply weathered volcanic rocks, usually basalt.

FACT FILE

The incredibly rich, 1926 discovery of gold at Edie Creek, in Papua New Guinea, became one of the biggest alluvial dredging operations in the world.

NATURAL RESOURCES IN OCEANIA

The lure of gold and other raw materials also attracted Europeans to the Pacific. The discovery of gold on New Zealand's South Island in the 1850s boosted the population. Interest in gold mining faded in the 1920s, but rising gold prices in the mid-1970s reignited mining investment, exploration, and production. Full-scale mining did not begin in New Guinea until the discovery of gold there in the 1880s.

In the 1910s and 1920s, chromite mined on New Caledonia constituted 40 percent of the island's economy and 25 percent of the world's supply of chromite. In the twenty-first century, mineral riches are being tapped throughout Oceania. Natural gas and oil are found in Papua New Guinea, New Zealand, the Solomon Islands, Vanuatu, Fiji, and Tonga; coal, iron ore, and hydropower in New Zealand; phosphate on Tonga and Kiribati; cobalt on French Polynesia; and nickel in New Caledonia.

Nauru's legacy of mining phosphate has created a moonlike landscape.

The mining of natural minerals brings much needed foreign currency into the economy of Oceania, but the sustainability of the resources and the effects their exploitation has on the natural landscape and the lifestyle of local inhabitants have raised considerable environmental and social concerns. On Nauru, phosphate has been mined by German, British, and Australian companies throughout the twentieth century, bringing unimagined wealth to its inhabitants. The mining of phosphate, however, has removed much of the island's land surface, displacing a traditional agricultural economy. In the process, the people of Nauru have become dependent on imports, especially the high sugar and fat content in processed foods, leading to alarming rates of diabetes. Forty percent of Nauru's population of 12,800 people have been diagnosed with diabetes.

FACT FILE

In 2004, the supply of phosphate—the economic base of Nauru—was exhausted, leaving Nauru dependent on aid from Australia.

Great tracts of unspoiled rain forests are also being depleted. The debate over unsustainable forests and the clearing of forests for paper products in Australia keeps a political focus on the problem. But elsewhere, the concerns of conservationists are largely ignored. The Solomon Islands have already been stripped bare of their forests. A similar fate is now confronting 34,594,000 acres (14 million ha) in Papua New Guinea. The forests are being harvested by international companies, whose actions are tolerated by

Logging in the Western Province of Papua New Guinea.

the government of Papua New Guinea because it is desperate for foreign income. The environmental consequences are telling. Run-off from sawmills and effluent from logging camps are polluting the river systems. Little regard is given to traditional hunting and fishing areas, native flora, or burial grounds. The companies are barely providing any infrastructure, and little of the economic benefit is going to the local landowners.

NATURAL RESOURCES IN ANTARCTICA

Early European exploitation of Antarctica was by whalers and sealers. Their rate of fishing soon put whale populations on the brink of extinction. Today, commercial fishing interests in Antarctic waters are mostly from Japan and Norway and focus on krill, finfish, cod, herring, and whiting. Once again, the amount of fish being taken (especially krill, an essential part of the food chain for whales and other marine species) is raising concern about damage to Antarctica's ecosystem.

Exploration in Antarctica has revealed deposits of iron ore, chromium, copper, gold, nickel, platinum, and other minerals, and coal and hydrocarbons have been found in small uncommercial quantities. Antarctica's distance from world markets and its hostile environment, however, have meant that little economic development has taken place. The International Protocol on Environmental Protection to the Antarctic Treaty protects Antarctica from mineral exploitation as well as covering areas of marine pollution until 2050.

● ● ● ● ● ● ● ▶ IN FOCUS: Mining in Papua New Guinea

In Papua New Guinea, mining accounts for one-third of government revenue and 70 percent of export earnings. The OK Tedi Mine is the largest source of copper, processing 100,000 tons (90,720 tonnes) of ore per day. Copper makes up only 1–2 percent of this ore and the remainder, together with waste rock, is disposed of in rivers, land sites, or the ocean. Other environmental damage is caused by the impact of mining on the immediate land— it is estimated that the depth of the open pit at OK Tedi will be 4,265 feet (1,300 m) by 2010—as well as the use of land for supporting mining infrastructure, such as processing mills, workshops, accommodations, offices, and villages. This environmental damage has had a devastating effect on the traditional culture and agricultural practices of people who live nearby, and it proceeds despite their protests.

The OK Tedi copper mine has had serious effects on the environment.

6. THE ECONOMIES OF AUSTRALIA, ANTARCTICA, AND THE PACIFIC

*I*N THE TWENTY-FIRST CENTURY, AUSTRALIA IS A HIGHLY INDUSTRIAL-ized nation with a prosperous Western-style capitalist economy. Its GDP per capita is on a par with dominant West European economies. Economic development in Oceania has been less bright, however, and it is severely affected by such factors as size, limited resources, distance from markets and suppliers, and changes in the global economy.

AUSTRALIA'S ECONOMY

Since the nineteenth century, the Australian economy has been based on agriculture, especially wool, meat, and wheat, and then mining. This focus has changed in the last fifty years, however, and now the Australian workforce is primarily engaged in secondary production—notably vehicles, medicine and pharmaceuticals, and computer and telecommunication equipment—and the service sectors, such as education and tourism.

Today, Australia's main industries are mining (particularly coal, crude petroleum, gold, iron ore, and aluminum), manufacturing, agriculture, and tourism. Wool remains an important commodity and represents 25 percent of the world's wool production. Ninety-five percent of Australian wool is exported to Japan and Europe. Both agricultural products and

Aluminum being loaded onto cargo ships for export. Western Australia is one of the world's largest suppliers of aluminum.

energy and mineral resources are exported, with Japan (18.5 percent) and the United States (9.6 percent) the largest revenue markets. Australia's main imports are machinery and transportation equipment, computer and telecommunication components, crude oil, and petroleum products. Imports come predominantly from the United States (18.3 percent), Japan (12.3 percent), and China (10.1 percent).

Other factors have also contributed to Australia's economic strength. They include increasing trade within its immediate Asia-Pacific region and the development of new areas of growth, such as tourism. The Australia-United States Free Trade Agreement, negotiated with the United States in 2004, is also expected to have a positive impact on the economy by eliminating import taxes and encouraging trade between the two countries.

OCEANIA'S ECONOMY

Agriculture, especially dairy products and meat, has been the foundation of New Zealand's economy. Indeed, it has been called "the largest farm in the world." Britain has historically been New Zealand's largest trading partner, although new partners have been sought since the 1970s.

By the 1980s, New Zealand had reformed its economic base. It is now a heavily industrialized economy with a global market, with interests in food processing, wood and paper products, mining, and textiles, as well as a continued reliance on agricultural trade. New

Sheep on a farm in New Zealand's North Island.

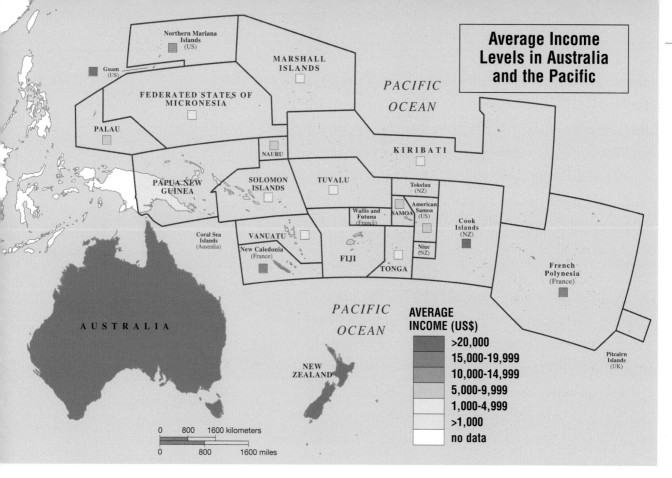

Average Income Levels in Australia and the Pacific

AVERAGE INCOME (US$)	
	>20,000
	15,000-19,999
	10,000-14,999
	5,000-9,999
	1,000-4,999
	>1,000
	no data

0   800   1600 kilometers

0   800   1600 miles

Small landholders, such as these Samoan village women, are being encouraged to plant high-yield crops, such as peanuts.

Zealand lamb and wool products are recognized internationally for their high quality. Today, New Zealand's main export trading partners are Australia (22 percent), the United States (15.6 percent), and Japan (11.5 percent).

Most people elsewhere in Oceania continue to live in rural and fishing communities, often in small villages with limited opportunities for employment. The economies of the Oceanic Islands are heavily influenced by ecological factors. Other factors include the availability of arable land, the size of the work force, and the financial potential of each island-nation. Political instability and low foreign investment also play a role in restricting economic growth.

Apart from a small manufacturing sector that primarily processes agricultural products and textiles, subsistence farming and fishing form the bulk of Oceania's economies. American Samoa has only 5 percent of arable land along its coastal plains, while Micronesia relies on agriculture for 50 percent of its domestic economy.

Fiji, with one of the region's most developed economies, is endowed with forests, minerals, and fish resources. Yet with only 12 percent arable land, it still has a large subsistence sector, with 26 percent of the population living below the poverty line. Agriculture (particularly sugar) represents 17 percent of the economy; industry (small cottage textile industries and larger mining enterprises) represents 25 percent; and services (particularly tourism) another 56 percent.

The Cook Islands rely economically on agriculture, mainly copra and citrus fruit, and the manufacturing of textiles. Their economic growth is hindered by geographic isolation, the lack of natural resources, and periodic natural disasters, such as typhoons. Consequently, the Cook Islands are reliant on foreign aid, particularly from New Zealand and, to a lesser extent, Australia.

Colonial links have been economically useful for some island-nations. French Polynesia has hosted a large French military base since 1962 and has received a large influx of foreign capital. It continues to profit from development agreements with France aimed principally at creating new businesses and strengthening social services. Similarly, American Samoa benefits heavily from its link with the United States.

FACT FILE

In 2003, Australia was the largest provider of foreign aid in Oceania, giving US$352 million to Papua New Guinea and another US$297 million to the Pacific Islands. The money provides assistance for economic reform and better government administration, education and training, health care, and better management of natural resources and the environment.

The French government has spent millions of US$ maintaining its nuclear program in the Pacific

But dependence on more developed countries is not always beneficial. In 1979, the Federated States of Micronesia fell under U.S. administration and achieved independence in 1986. As a consequence, it has become overly dependent on financial aid from the United States, which has pledged US$3.5 billion (approximately 40 percent of Micronesia's GDP) between 1986 and 2023. Unemployment is at 16 percent, and 26.7 percent of its population lives below the poverty line.

TOURISM

The one area of economic growth that is benefiting both Australia and Oceania is tourism. In 2001, when 4.8 million visitors contributed US$13 billion to the Australian economy (11.2 percent of its total export earnings), the tourism industry employed 6 percent of Australia's workforce.

Each year, growing numbers of tourists from Europe, Australia, Asia, and North America visit Oceania. The number of tourists is growing by 10 percent each year. In 2003, more than one million people visited the South Pacific Islands alone. Fiji, French Polynesia, New Caledonia, and Samoa are the most popular destinations in the region.

Pacific Islands are increasingly focusing on tourism as the basis of their economic development. Smaller nations have been developing niche marketing in adventure, cultural, and eco tourism. For some island-nations, it is payingoff , with tourism in North Mariana Islands and Samoa constituting 25 percent of their economies. Tourism growth across the region, however, is hindered by inadequate air connections and the lack of sufficient facilities, such as freshwater and sanitation. Another

FACT FILE

It is anticipated that the number of tourists to Australia will double by 2013.

Western Samoa's Lalomanu Beach is typical of the island paradises that are attracting increasing numbers of tourists to Oceania.

problem is the regular devastation of tourism facilities by extreme climatic occurrences, such as cyclones. When Cyclone Ivy hit Vanuatu in February 2004, it disrupted international flights and forced the evacuation of one thousand residents from the main towns and the closure of some resorts.

Seasonal employment and an economic overdependence on tourism at the expense of traditional forms of income are some of the detrimental effects of this industry. The economic downturn in Asia during the late 1990s had a major impact on Micronesia, which was very dependent on Asian visitors. Tourism may also present challenges to traditional cultures. In addition, increasing numbers of tourists may be damaging to the natural environment.

FACT FILE

Tourism to Antarctica has become a thriving business, with more than 13,000 tourists during the 2002–2003 season.

• • • • ▶ IN FOCUS: Tourism in Antarctica

Commercial tourism to Antarctica began in the 1950s, first by cruise ships and then by sightseeing flights from Australia and New Zealand. In 1969, the M/S *Lindbald Explorer* was the first passenger cruise ship designed specifically for carrying tourists to Antarctica. "Flight-seeing," or flying at a low altitude over Antarctica without landing, continues to be popular, despite the 1979 crash of a New Zealand airplane into Mount Erebus that killed 257 people.

Tourism in Antarctica is controlled by the Protocol on Environmental Protection of the Antarctic Treaty, which was adopted in 1991 to ensure the protection of the environment, and the International Association of Antarctica Tour Operators, which promotes safe and environmentally responsible tourism. Authorities are concerned, however, that they cannot monitor the rapidly increasing rate of tourism and avert ecological damage.

Ecotourists in Antarctica admire Adélie penguins.

7. Australia, Antarctica, and the Pacific in the World

Most nations in the Pacific region are too small to play a role in world affairs, with the exception of Australia and, to a lesser extent, New Zealand. Yet their history of European colonization has meant that Australia and the island-nations of Oceania have been strongly influenced by the cultures and economies of Europe and the United States.

The region's relationship with the rest of the world has accelerated since the middle of the twentieth century. During World War II, the military forces of the United States, Australia, and New Zealand fought together against Japan in the Pacific. The presence of the Allied and Japanese forces on many Pacific islands was to have an impact on traditional cultures. In Papua New Guinea, in particular, the indigenous population played a key role in assisting Allied troops during the war. In addition, defense, cultural, and economic ties between Australia and the United States were strengthened as a result of the war. In 1951, the regional

Trading on the floor of the Sydney Stock Exchange.

FACT FILE

The Australian trading day for the stock market is truly global—it spans the close of business in the United States and the opening of business in Europe, while coinciding with business in Asia.

defense ANZUS Treaty was signed between Australia, New Zealand, and the United States, signaling a new era of international relations within the region.

Today, the impact of global trade and the influence of global media have meant that the cultures and economies of these countries are increasingly bound up in worldwide developments.

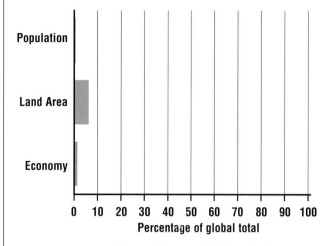

Australia, Antarctica, and the Pacific Compared with the Rest of the World

Population

Land Area

Economy

0 10 20 30 40 50 60 70 80 90 100
Percentage of global total

Source: United Nations; World Bank; Britannica Book of the Year 2004

AUSTRALIA AND NEW ZEALAND AND THE WORLD

Australia's international relations were traditionally linked to those of Britain, but after 1945 its security in the region has been increasingly aligned with the United States. Australian forces have played a role in international conflicts in Korea, Vietnam, the Gulf War, and Iraq. They have also been involved in United Nations peacekeeping activities, including playing a leading role in East Timor.

Australia's engagement with the world has also been increasingly concerned with the region of Asia, especially in relation to trade. Between 1983 and 2002, foreign investment in Australia grew from US$63.4 billion to US$177.5 billion, of which 28.7 percent came from American sources and 10.4 percent from Japanese, Hong Kong, and Chinese sources.

Australia has taken a leading role within the Pacific region, particularly in ensuring political and economic stability. It is the major provider of foreign aid and assistance programs to the

More than 1,000 Australian troops and civilians helped in the rebuilding of East Timor after it gained independence from Indonesia in 2002.

An additional 1.2 million tourists watched athletes from more than 100 countries compete at the Olympic Games in Sydney.

underdeveloped countries in the region. Australian aid includes funds for educational, health, and economic development programs.

Like Australia, New Zealand was historically linked to Britain and its foreign policy but more recently has given priority to its immediate region. New Zealand has been a strong opponent of nuclear testing in the Pacific by the United States. As a consequence of this objection, New Zealand withdrew from active participation in the ANZUS Treaty in 1986. New Zealand is an important member in Pacific-wide economic and cultural organizations and developments.

Tourism to New Zealand is also growing, and the country's scenic beauty and developed infrastructure has made it a desirable and highly competitive location for international film production. Peter Jackson's *Lord of the Rings* film trilogy—filmed in New Zealand—has given the country an international profile.

ANTARCTICA AND THE WORLD
Signed on December 1, 1959, the Antarctic Treaty established the legal framework for the management of Antarctica. Today, forty-five nations are treaty members. Consultative, or voting,

members include the seven nations that claim portions of Antarctica as national territory (Argentina, Australia, Chile, New Zealand, the United Kingdom, France, and Norway) and 20 nonclaimant nations. Antarctica is administered through meetings of the consultative member nations. Decisions from these meetings are carried out by these member nations within their areas, in accordance with their own national laws.

INTERNATIONAL CHALLENGES

In recent years, the "War against Terror" has been fought on numerous fronts across the Asia-Pacific region. Terrorist bombings were directed against Australia in 2002, when many Australians vacationing in Indonesia were killed in an attack on a nightclub in Bali. The Australian Embassy in Jakarta was also bombed in 2004. As a consequence, Australian authorities are co-operating internationally to monitor and prevent terrorist activities.

The Australian Navy clears mines from Umm Qasr Port in Iraq in March 2003.

Enforcement agencies in Australia and New Zealand are concerned about the region's increasing problems in enforcing the control of national borders and preventing illegal immigration. The policing of illegal immigration in the region involves cooperation with authorities in Asia, Europe, and the United States. The increasing incidence of crime in the Pacific region, including the trafficking of illegal drugs, is also an issue of growing concern. Regional responses to these activities have again been conducted in association with international law enforcement bodies.

ENVIRONMENTAL ISSUES IN A GLOBAL CONTEXT

Climate change is a global phenomenon with lasting and adverse consequences. It has been predicted that because of the delicate and unique environments of Australia and Oceania, the effect of climate change will particularly affect the economic developments within the region. There is concern that increased

FACT FILE

The Pacific Ocean contains other island-nations that are not part of Oceania. Indonesia, the Philippines, and Japan are located in the continent of Asia. The islands that lie in the eastern Pacific Ocean near North America and South America are parts of those continents. The nations that border the Pacific Ocean are referred to as being part of the Pacific Rim.

melting of the polar ice caps, which will lead to rising sea levels, poses a long-term threat to small island-nations in Oceania and the coastal areas of Australia and New Zealand.

The United Nations Framework on Climate Change has established the Kyoto Protocol, which aims to reduce the amount of greenhouse gases that are emitted through the use of energy in industry and agriculture and the use of motor vehicles. New Zealand has ratified the Kyoto Protocol, and its government is committed to environmentally sustainable policies. Australia, like the United States, has not ratified the Kyoto Protocol but has allocated funding to reduce the emission of greenhouse gases and to develop new and efficient environmentally sensitive technologies.

The Pacific Islands Forum aims to enhance the economic and social well being of the peoples of the South Pacific through cooperation between governments and international agencies.

REGIONAL COOPERATION

The nations of Oceania have united to represent their broad interests in international affairs. The Pacific Islands Forum (formerly the South Pacific Forum 1971–2000) meets annually to discuss regional trade and security. In 2003, the Forum voted to intervene in the Solomon Islands where significant deterioration of law and order was threatening the stability of the community. Since 1994, the Forum has had observer status at the United Nations and at meetings of the Asia-Pacific Economic Cooperation (APEC).

APEC was founded in 1989 to assist economic growth in the Asia-Pacific region. It has twenty-one "member economies," including Australia, New Zealand, and Papua New Guinea, as well as the United States, Japan, the People's Republic of China, and other nations in the Pacific Rim and Asia. Together, these member economies account for almost 50 percent of the world's trade and more than one-third of the world's population.

Other regional organizations include the South Pacific Commission, established in 1947 by European powers with interests in Oceania to provide development assistance; the Tourism Council of the South Pacific; and the South Pacific Regional Environment Program. Another two hundred regional organizations link interests across business, the arts, communications, and education.

•••••••▶ IN FOCUS: Nuclear testing

One of the strongest cooperative developments has been the response to nuclear testing in the South Pacific. First the Americans in the 1950s, then the French until the 1980s, tested nuclear weapons at remote atolls over which they had possession. In August 1985, eight members of the South Pacific Forum signed the Treaty of Raratonga, requiring all nations to stop testing or storing nuclear weapons in the South Pacific and from dumping nuclear waste there. The major nuclear powers signed and ratified the protocols by 1997.

Greenpeace's ship _Rainbow Warrior_, used in antinuclear protests, was sabotaged with bombs by French spies on July 10, 1985, with one crew member drowned.

8. WILDLIFE IN AUSTRALIA, ANTARCTICA, AND THE PACIFIC

THE GEOLOGICAL SEPARATION OF LANDMASSES AND THE ISOLATED processes of species evolution over millions of years have resulted in the region's diversity of unique flora and fauna.

Grey kangaroos can jump up to 30 feet (9 m) in a single bound.

FACT FILE

Kangaroos are a protected species, but annual assessments determine whether legal harvesting is necessary to maintain their numbers at a sustainable level.

ANIMAL LIFE

Australia's unique fauna include monotremes (egg-laying mammals), such as the platypus and echidna. Also found only in Australia is the dingo, a large hunting dog that came from Asia to Australia approximately 5,000 years ago. Among the 16 marsupial families native to Australia are possums, tree-dwelling koalas, wombats, kangaroos, and wallabies. Australia is home to 50 species of kangaroos, the largest two being grey and red kangaroos. In 2003, the kangaroo population was approximately 28 million—with 90 percent being red and grey kangaroos.

More than 360 of Australia's 750 vibrant bird species are unique to the continent. Australia's largest native bird, the emu, stands 6.5 feet (2 m) tall and is found throughout Australia. Also distinct to Australia are honeyeaters, bowerbirds, and frogmouths, plus an array of 50 species of brilliantly colored parrots. These include parakeets, lorikeets, cockatoos, and galahs. Australian customs authorities guard against the illegal smuggling of live parrots out of the country.

Flightless kagu birds in the rain forests of New Caledonia.

The absence of land dwelling mammals from New Zealand and other parts of Oceania allowed the evolution of a diversified range of exotic birds. A number of these birds are flightless, because they had no need to fly away from predators. These species include kakapos, kiwis, and moas (now extinct) in New Zealand and the forest-dwelling kagu in New Caledonia. New Guinea's extraordinarily plumed "bird of paradise" lives in the lowland and mid-mountain forests. Its spectacular colors serve as attractors during mating season and also function as protective camouflage amidst the colors of the forest.

Marine mammals, including several species of whales and dolphins, are common in the waters of the Pacific Ocean. In New Zealand and Australia, whale watching has become an important tourist attraction. Many species of sharks also live in area waters. Sometimes, they pose a danger to swimmers and surfers, and a "shark patrol" operates on many popular Australian beaches, calling everyone to shore when sharks are sighted.

PLANT LIFE

Some of Australia and New Zealand's flora are also remnants of Gondwanaland. Huge kauri and southern beech, broad-leaf evergreens, and conifers are found in the dense rain forests of New Zealand. The rain forests

FACT FILE

Of the 20,000 species of plants in Australia, 17,000 are unique to the continent. Eighty to ninety percent of all the mammals, insects, and reptiles in Australia also are found nowhere else on Earth.

FACT FILE

Australia has more species of poisonous snakes than any other continent. The most venomous snake in the world, the Eastern Taipan, lives in Australia's desert interior.

New Zealand's kauri are among the world's greatest trees, reaching heights of 164 feet (50 m).

of Northern Queensland contain flowering plants, palms, and laurels, and more than five hundred species of eucalyptus, while the temperate rain forests of Tasmania have myrtle beech, tree ferns, and moss.

CONSERVATION

In Australia and New Zealand, conservation of natural environments and animal and plant species has been aided by international organizations, such as Greenpeace, as well as national government and non-government organizations. Community protest has drawn attention to conservation issues and was successful in preventing the damming of the Franklin River in Tasmania in the 1980s. There are now many national parks in Australia and New Zealand. Classified World Heritage sites in Australia include national parks at Uluru/Ayers Rock and at Kakadu in the Northern Territory.

WILDLIFE IN ANTARCTICA

Each season, about 100 million birds breed along Antarctica's coastline and on offshore islands, including species of petrels, terns, and the wandering albatross. Four species of penguins live on Antarctica. During winter, male Emperor Penguins, protected by a thick layer of insulating fat, huddle close together in a large group to help keep warm the eggs that the males balance on their feet.

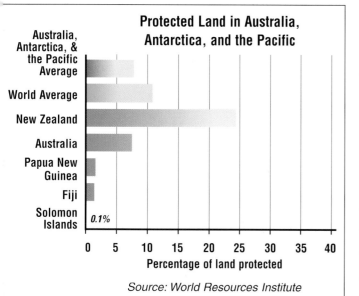

Protected Land in Australia, Antarctica, and the Pacific

Category	Percentage of land protected
Australia, Antarctica, & the Pacific Average	~8
World Average	~11
New Zealand	~24
Australia	~8
Papua New Guinea	~2
Fiji	~2
Solomon Islands	0.1%

Source: World Resources Institute

Chemicals released into the atmosphere have caused a huge hole in the ozone layer over Antarctica that is already endangeing wildlife. Icebergs are breaking away from the coast of

Antarctica, preventing colonies of more than 100,000 penguins from reaching their breeding grounds. Scientists fear that Adélie penguins in the southern part of the Ross Sea will not survive.

Despite the extreme climate, a surprising number of plants thrive in Antarctica, particularly many species of lichen, mosses, and fungi, and more than 700 species of algae.

Adélie penguins hunt for food in the open waters of the Antarctic.

●●●● ▶ IN FOCUS: The Great Barrier Reef

The Great Barrier Reef lies off the coast of Queensland, Australia. It is made up of many tiny organisms called coral polyps joined together by their outer skeletons. The reef is home to 1,500 species of brilliantly colored tropical fish and 400 types of hard and soft coral. Coral bleaching is increasing, as are predators, such as poisonous crown-of-thorns starfish. Since the 1960s, nesting loggerhead turtles have declined by 50–80 percent, while dugong (a marine mammal that lives mainly on plants and

is also known as a sea cow) populations are nearly extinct. Humans are the reef's greatest threat. Recreational divers who harm coral, pollution, and fishing with chemicals or the use of explosives to increase a catch all pose threats. In July 2004, however, the Great Barrier Reef was declared a Maritime National Park, effectively ending commercial fishing on large sections of the reef.

The coral and marine life of the Great Barrier Reef attracts thousands of divers annually.

9. THE FUTURE OF AUSTRALIA, ANTARCTICA, AND THE PACIFIC

*T*HERE ARE MANY IMMEDIATE AND LONG-TERM CHALLENGES FOR Australia, Antarctica, and Oceania during the twenty-first century. The role of regional and international cooperation is increasingly important. The remote nations of the Pacific, while maintaining their unique identities, are now part of global economic and cultural processes.

REGIONAL STABILITY

Both Australia and New Zealand have stable economies and political systems and are eager to promote stability within the wider region. Most Pacific island-nations have achieved independence from former colonial governments. Democratic systems of government have been adopted by these nations, but in many cases, younger generations are applying pressure for further political reform. This pressure has highlighted social divisions and may conflict with traditional systems of social hierarchy and chiefly rule. In Papua New Guinea and New Caledonia, political unrest has occurred as particular ethnic groups have sought independence from the ruling government.

Foreign aid has been critical for the economic stability of many Oceanic nations. While Australia is the major contributor of foreign aid in the Pacific, the emphasis remains on sustainable development and the need to develop new and ongoing sources of revenue.

On April 2, 2000, 80,000 plastic "hands" were planted in the sands of Sydney's Coogee Beach to show support by Australians for reconciliation between indigenous and non-indigenous Australians.

Other issues, such as the adequate provision of education, housing, and health services and the demands of the labor market, require attention. So does the problem of widespread poverty in many underdeveloped Oceanic islands. In wealthy countries, such as Australia, the gap between those with higher and lower incomes is widening.

Population increases have created an urgent problem for some Oceanic nations where land and resources are limited. The situation is different, however, in Australia and New Zealand, where both countries have a low birth rate and their populations are growing older. Here, the economic and social implications are serious, including rising costs to governments in providing "old age" pensions. The number of immigrants allowed into Australia each year remains widely debated. So, too, does the question of the rights and needs of Australia's and New Zealand's indigenous peoples.

While scientists continue to explore Antarctica, international disputes over territorial claims by various nations with direct and indirect interests remain a preoccupation of the members of the Antarctic Treaty.

THE ULTIMATE CHALLENGE

The management of the environment looms as the greatest challenge facing Antarctica, Australia, and Oceanic nations. Long-term concerns include pollution, the depletion of the ozone layer and its climatic consequences, and the over-exploitation of the region's rich resources. The control of environmental damage by introduced species and the need to halt the possible extinction of many species of plant and animal life in the region also needs addressing.

Increasing costs of living are forcing Australian retirees back into the workforce and placing a strain on the government provision of pensions and heath facilities.

STATISTICAL COMPENDIUM

Nation	Area (sq miles)	Population (2003)	Urbanization (% population) 2003	Life expectancy at birth 2002 (in years)	GDP per capita (US $) 2002	Percentage of population under 15 years 2003	Percentage of population over 65 years 2003
American Samoa	77	62,000	90.3	N/A	N/A	N/A	N/A
Australia	2,965,368	19,731,000	92	79.1	28,260	20	12
Fiji	7,053	839,000	51.7	69.6	5,440	33	4
French Polynesia	1,544	244,000	52.1	74.0	28,020***	30	6
Guam	209	163,000	93.7	78.0	N/A	34	7
Kiribati	313	88,000	47.3	63.0	N/A	39	3
Marshall Islands	70	53,000	66.3	65.0***	N/A	N/A	N/A
Micronesia	271	109,000	29.3	69.0	N/A	36	4
Nauru	8	13,000	100.0	N/A	N/A	N/A	N/A
New Caledonia	7,170	228,000	61.2	74.0	25,200***	29	7
New Zealand	104,426	3,875,000	85.9	78.2	21,740	22	12
Northern Mariana Islands	184	79,000	94.2	N/A	N/A	N/A	N/A
Palau	188	20,000	68.6	70.0***	N/A	N/A	N/A
Papua New Guinea	178,656	5,711,000	13.2	57.4	2,270	41	2
Samoa	1,093	178,000	22.3	69.8	5,600	35	5
Solomon Islands	10,951	477,000	16.5	69.0	1,590	45	3
Tonga	290	104,000	33.4	68.4	6,850	33	9
Tuvalu	10	11,000	55.2	N/A	N/A	N/A	N/A
Vanuatu	4,705	212,000	22.8	68.6	2,890	41	3

*** Data from 2000   *Sources: UN Agencies, World Bank, Social Watch and Britannica*

GLOSSARY

Aborigines any of the indigenous peoples of Australia

Adaro a Melanesian mythical creature that is half human and half fish. It lives in the Sun and travels to Earth on rainbows.

allied in close association or joined by treaty or agreement. During World War II, the Allied forces were those who joined together to fight against Germany, Japan, Italy, Hungary, Romania, and Bulgaria.

alluvial plains a flat area built up over many thousands of years by deposits of river sediment, such as a delta or estuary

amalgamated joined together

artesian a reservoir of water lying under the earth's surface

atoll a coral island consisting of a ring-shaped coral reef enclosing a lagoon

canon in literature, a body of related books that are widely recognized

climate change the process of long-term changes to the world's climate

continental shelf an area of seabed that borders the shore of a continent and ends in a steep slope toward the deep ocean floor

coral the hard skeletons of sea animals that join together by the thousands to form reefs and, sometimes, islands

coral bleaching the loss of color in coral, brought on when environmental stressors cause the loss of microscopic plants that live in the coral and provide it with food

dominion a territory subject to the control of another nation

dormant in a state of temporary inactivity

dredging digging up soil from a river or other body of water

effluent the discharge of waste material, often of a pollutant, into the environment

emu a flightless Australian bird

erosion the wearing away of a substance, such as soil, from wind and/or water

federated united in a league or political organization with a central government and a number of separate states that maintain control of their internal affairs

GDP (Gross Domestic Product) the market value of all goods and services produced within a country over a set period of time

geographic South Pole the point where Earth's axis of rotation intersects the surface

Gondwanaland an ancient land mass in the Southern Hemisphere that broke up about 600 million years ago to form Antarctica, South America, Africa, and Australia

greenhouse gases atmospheric gases, such as carbon dioxide and methane, that trap heat radiating from Earth's surface and contribute to global warming and climate change

indentured being bound to work for another person for a period of time

Indian Subcontinent the peninsula of South Asia, comprised of India, Bangladesh, Pakistan, and Sri Lanka

indigenous having originated in and living, growing, being produced, or occurring naturally in a particular area or environment

infrastructure the systems and public works that allow communication and/or help people and the economy to function, including roads, railroads, electricity, and phone lines

irrigation the artificial watering of farmland

kinship the network of family relationships

krill the common name to some eighty-five species of small free-swimming crustaceans called euphausiids

magnetic South Pole the point where the field line of Earth's magnetic field points directly into the earth. Here the compass points north. The Magnetic South Point is located in the Antarctic Ocean.

Maori indigenous peoples of New Zealand

marsupials mammals that carry and suckle their newborn young in a stomach pouch on the outside of the mother's body

missionaries people sent to a foreign land to spread a religion or do social work

monsoon a seasonal wind in Southeast Asia that brings heavy rains

outcroppings parts of rock formations that appear above the surface of surrounding land or sea

penal colony a prison, or jail, often on an island from which it is difficult to escape

poverty line a level of income below which a person or family is considered poor by government standards

ratified the formal approval of an agreement, such as a treaty

salinity the remains of salt deposits in the soil that deplete its agricultural usefulness

solar radiation the amount of radiation or energy received from the Sun at a given point

terra nullius Latin for "empty land" or "no man's land." The principle used by the English to justify colonizing Australian land not settled or cultivated by indigenous peoples.

FURTHER INFORMATION

BOOKS TO READ:

Bocknek, Jonathan. *Antarctica: The Last Wilderness.* Understanding Global Issues (series). Mankato, MN: Smart Apple Media, 2003.

Ercelawn, Ayesha. *New Zealand.* Countries of the World (series). Milwaukee: Gareth Stevens, 2001.

Gascoigne, Ingrid. *Papua New Guinea.* Cultures of the World (series). New York: Benchmark Books, 1998.

North, Peter. *Australia.* Countries of the World (series). Milwaukee: Gareth Stevens, 1998.

Pelta, Kathy. *Rediscovering Easter Island.* How History is Invented (series). Minneapolis: Lerner Publishing Group, 2001.

Steele, Philip. *Sydney.* Great Cities of the World (series). Milwaukee: World Almanac Library, 2004.

USEFUL WEB SITES:

www.70south.com/home
This site gives the history of and up-to-date news and information about all matters relating to Antarctica.

www.gbrmpa.gov.au/index.html
This Australian government Web site for the Great Barrier Reef Marine Park Authority provides an enormous amount of information on and pictures of the reef. Education section offers student activities and lets readers "explore" the reef.

www.govt.nz/en/aboutnz/
This government site provides access to information about New Zealand's history, people, culture, and wildlife.

www.odci.gov/cia/publications/factbook/
This CIA Web site gives facts and figures for Australia, New Zealand, Antarctica, and many of the island-nations of Oceania.

INDEX

ABOUT THE AUTHOR

Kate Darian-Smith is Professor of Australian Studies and History at the University of Melbourne, Australia. She is the Director of the Australian Centre, an interdisciplinary research and teaching department that focuses on Australia's human and natural environments within their international context. She previously taught in universities in the United Kingdom and the United States. She is the author and editor of several books on Australian history and society, including a number of books written for young people about Australia and the Asia-Pacific region.